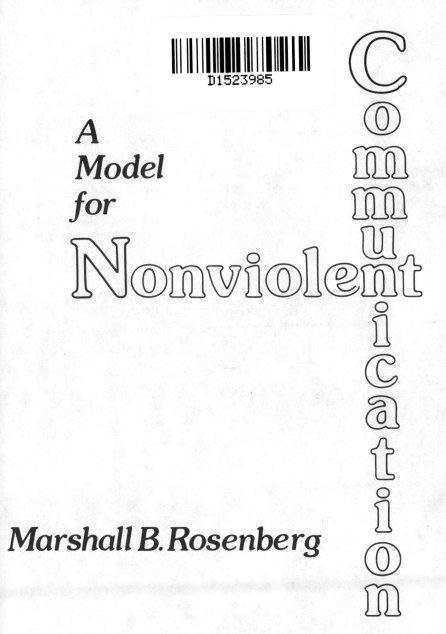

A
Model
for

Nonviolent

Communication

Marshall B. Rosenberg

New Society Publishers

New Society Publishers is a collective of Movement for a New Society, a network of small groups working for fundamental social change through nonviolent action.

This pamphlet has been reviewed by the Mid-Atlantic Regional Service Collective of Movement for a New Society (MNS), acting as the representatives of the MNS Network. It has our sponsorship as a valuable piece of literature, with perspectives worthy of consideration and discussion. The opinions stated herein do not necessarily represent agreed-upon positions of either the Mid-Atlantic Regional Service Collective or the MNS Network as a whole.

Marshall B. Rosenberg can be reached:
c/o The Center for Nonviolent Communication
3229 Bordeaux, Sherman, Texas 75090
(214) 893-3886

TABLE OF CONTENTS

Chapter One

Introduction

Do you dream the same dreams I dream?
I wonder if we value the same things.
I love the joy
and the tenderness
finding a new soulmate brings.

Do you dream of a world where touching
enriches, nurtures, and soothes;
and the people are willing
to abstain from all killing
and Arabs dance the Hora with the Jews?

Do you dream of a world where each person
is only an end, never just a cog
and mistakes don't require
damnation or hellfire
just some loving dialogue?

1

I'm writing this manual to make available some communication skills that I believe empower us to exchange resources and resolve differences nonviolently.

The skills to be described are those necessary to offer and receive "empowering evaluations." In contrast to evaluations which influence people to act on the basis of fear or guilt, "empowering evaluations" provide opportunities for people to nurture, educate, and protect one another and are the nucleus of communication necessary to exchange resources and resolve differences nonviolently.

Empowering evaluations express:
    What we are observing (the subject of Chapter 2)
    What we are feeling (the subject of Chapter 3)
    What we are valuing (the subject of Chapter 4)
    What we are requesting (the subject of Chapter 5)

Receiving "empowering evaluations" will be the subject of Chapter 6.

Chapter Two

What we are observing

I can handle your telling me
 what I did or didn't do.
And I can handle your interpretations
 but, please, don't mix the two.

If you want to confuse any issue
 I can tell you how to do it:
Mix together what I do
 with how you react to it.

Tell me that you're disappointed
 with the unfinished chores you see,
But calling me "irresponsible"
 is no way to motivate me.

And tell me that you're feeling hurt
 when I say, "No", to your advances,
But calling me a frigid man
 won't increase your future chances.

The first piece of information in empowering evaluations describes what we are observing.

If people are behaving in ways we don't like and we'd like to influence them to change their behavior; or if people are behaving in ways we do like and we'd like to express our appreciation, I believe it is to our advantage to clearly express what we're reacting to without mixing in any evaluation. Mixing together our evaluation with what we are observing often provokes misinterpretation and defensiveness. For example, I recall a mother and her fifteen year-old daughter who came to see me for counseling. In the course of our conversation I asked the mother to tell me one thing her daughter was doing that she would like to change. The mother said, "She is totally irresponsible." The daughter was quick to react to the statement saying, "That's not so." I pointed out to the mother that I had asked what the daughter *did*, not what she thought the daughter was for doing it. The mother then responded, "She thinks she's the only one in the family." Again the daughter said, "That's not so." Again I pointed out to the mother that she was giving me her evaluation but not telling me what the daughter did. The mother thought for a moment and said, "That's hard to do. Everything that comes to my mind is an evaluation."

I sympathized with the mother. Mixing up what I observe people doing with how I evaluate them for doing it is also easy for me to do. Part of the problem is the type of language we have learned which Wendell Johnson describes this way:

> Our language is an imperfect instrument created by ancient and ignoant men. It is an animistic language that invites us to talk about stability and constants, about similarities and normal and kinds, about magical transformations, quick cures, simple problems, and final solutions. Yet the world we try to symbolize with this language is a world of process, change, differences, dimensions, functions, relationships, growths, interactions, developing, learning, coping, complexity. And the mismatch of our ever-changing world and our relatively static language forms is part of our problem.
>
> *(1972)*

4

In Table 1 I have summarized some of the most frequent ways I observe people confusing their observations and evaluations.

Table 1
Frequent ways of confusing what is being observed with one's evaluation of what is being observed.

	Example of confusion of observation and evaluation.	Example of separating observation and evaluation.
1. Use of verb "to be" without statements indicating evaluator is aware an evaluation is taking place.	You are too generous.	When you give all your lunch money to others, I think you are too generous.
2. Use of verbs with evaluative connotations.	Doug procrastinates.	Doug does not study for exams until the night before.
3. Implication that one's inferences about another person's thoughts, feelings, intentions or desires are the only possible inferences.	He won't get his work in.	He didn't get his work in. (or, He said, "I won't get it in.")
4. Confusion of prediction with certainty.	If you don't eat balanced meals you won't grow as much.	I'm worried that if you don't eat balanced meals you won't grow as much.
5. Failure to be specific about person, place.	Blacks don't cut their grass or repair their houses.	I have not seen the black family at 1679 Ross cut their lawn or fix the shingles on the roof.
6. Use of words denoting ability or inability to act without indicating that evaluation is being made.	Hank Smith cannot hit Big League pitching.	Hank Smith's lifetime batting average is .129.
7. Use of adjectives and adverbs in ways which do not signify that an evaluation has been made.	Jim is ugly.	Jim's looks don't appeal to me.

5

(Note: The words "always" and "never" and their synonyms are adverbs that are observations when used in the following way:

"Whenever I have observed Jack on the phone, he has spoken for at least thirty minutes."

"I cannot recall you *ever* writing to me."

Very often, however, the words are used as exaggerations to stress a point. For example, "You are always busy." My experience has been that when used as exaggerations they often provoke defensiveness rather than the response desired by the speaker.

The words, "frequently," and "seldom," and their synonyms are adverbs that often confuse observation and evaluation. Examples of how these might sound when observation and evaluation are separated are:

You seldom do what I want.	The last three times I initiated an activity you said you didn't want to.
He frequently comes over.	He comes over more often that I'd like.

I am providing an exercise for you to use if you'd like to determine whether or not we are communicating about how to keep our evaluations separate from the events we are evaluating. I'd like you to circle the items where you believe the speaker's statements reflect a separation of what is observed from the speaker's evaluation of what is being observed.

1. He is not very intelligent.

2. It is essential that you drink milk.

3. I am a shy person.

4. I sense that something good is going to happen to me.

5. She is conceited.

6. The facts indicate that we have to move quickly.

7. On the average I play golf three times each week and watch three golf tournaments each year.

8. I read in the psychiatrist's report that he was labeled "unstable."

9. He came soon after he called.

10. They are not a religious family.

11. He is a sexist.

12. She has pretty features.

13. When I was in the military the officers in my division acted in what I would call an authoritarian manner.

14. I know you didn't mean that.

15. He handles aggression immaturely.

16. He has atrocious eating habits.

17. He is overly emotional.

18. Last week when I came to work late he said, "What's the matter, can't you afford an alarm clock?"

19. She manipulates others.

20. He brags about his accomplishments.

Following are my responses with which to compare yours:

1. *I do not see the speaker separating the observed behavior from the evaluation of the behavior. To do so the speaker might have said, "In my estimation, he's not very intelligent," or "When he does not do what I say after I've shown him how three times, I start thinking of him as not very intelligent."*

2. *I do not see the speaker separating the observed behavior from the evaluation of the behavior. To do so the speaker might have said, "I believe it is essential that you drink milk," or "The January 6, 1970, issue of 'Health Today' lists health advantages to drinking milk."*

3. *I do not see the speaker separating the observed behavior from the evaluation of the behavior. To do so the speaker might have said, "When I go to parties, I feel frightened and don't talk to people."*

4. *I do see the speaker separating observed behavior from inner evaluation.*

5. *I do not see the speaker separating the observed behavior from the evaluation of the behavior. To do so the speaker might have said, "In my estimation she is conceited," or "When she doesn't say 'hello' to me I think of her as being conceited."*

6. *I do not see the speaker separating the observed behavior from the evaluation of the behavior. To do so the speaker might have said, "I would like to move more quickly," or "I interpret the facts as suggesting we move more quickly."*

7. *I do see the speaker separating observed behavior from inner evaluation.*

8. *I do see the speaker separating observed behavior from inner evaluation.*

9. *I do not see the speaker separating the observed behavior from the evaluation of the behavior. To do so the speaker might have said, "He came within five minutes after he called."*

10. *I do not see the speaker separating the observed behavior from the evaluation of the behavior. To do so the speaker might have said, "I have never observed them going to church or saying grace before meals."*

11. *I do not see the speaker separating the observed behavior from the evaluation of the behavior. To do so the speaker might have said, "I recall him saying that women were meant to stay home and raise babies."*

8

12. *I do not see the speaker separating the observed behavior from the evaluation of the behavior. To do so the speaker might have said, "I would describe her features as attractive."*

13. *I do see the speaker separating observed behavior from inner evaluation.*

14. *I do not see the speaker separating the observed behavior from the evaluation of the behavior. To do so the speaker might have said, "I'm guessing that you didn't mean that."*

15. *I do not see the speaker separating the observed behavior from the evaluation of the behavior. To do so the speaker might have said, "The last two times other children called him names, he hit them."*

16. *I do not see the speaker separating the observed behavior from the evaluation of the behavior. To do so the speaker might have said, "At supper last night he held his head within an inch of his bowl while eating his soup."*

17. *I do not see the speaker separating the observed behavior from the evaluation of the behavior. To do so the speaker might have said, "He cries at times that I don't," or "I'm uncomfortable with how much he cries."*

18. *I do see the speaker separating observed behavior from inner evaluation.*

19. *I do not see the speaker separating the observed behavior from the evaluation of the behavior. To do so the speaker might have said, "I interpreted her as giving compliments before asking for favors."*

20. *I do not see the speaker separating the observed behavior from the evaluation of the behavior. To do so the speaker might have said, "He took ten minutes to describe tournaments he won during our staff meeting."*

Chapter Three

What we are feeling

I grew up believing
what was expected of me
was to prove how strong
and violent I could be.

And I've been afraid to admit it
when I'm lonely, scared, or sad.
I thought feelings were weakness
and weakness was bad.

The second piece of information in empowering evaluations describes how we are feeling.

It has been my experience that when I express how I feel about what I'm observing others usually care abut my feelings and are motivated to cooperate with me. Conversely, if I diagnose or judge others they often become resistent and antagonistic.

Our feelings are the messengers of our values in the sense that they bring us messages telling us whether what is happening is what we want to be happening. Therefore, when we are alienated from our feelings we are alienated from our values.

Some of our feelings inform us about whether what is happening to us physically is what we want to be happening. Such feelings inform us whether we're feeling "hungry," "cold," "tired," etc. Some of our feelings inform us about whether we are as involved intellectually in what is happening as we'd like to be (e.g. "interested," "confused," "curious"). Some of our feelings tell us whether or not people are behaving as we'd like them to ("happy," "joyful," "frustrated," "disappointed"). Some of our feelings tell us we are judging others and ourselves ("angry," "guilty").

Table 2 contains a glossary of words for describing feelings. Some people have told me the list has been useful to them in increasing the vocabulary they have to express the complexity of human emotion we experience.

Table 2
Feelings likely to be present when wants are being satisfied

absorbed	aroused	complacent	eager
adventurous	astonished	composed	ecstatic
affection	blissful	concerned	effervescent
alert	breathless	confident	elated
alive	buoyant	contented	electrified
amazed	calm	cool	encouraged
amused	carefree	curious	energetic
animated	cheerful	dazzled	engrossed
appreciation	comfortable	delighted	enjoyment

enlivened	good-humored	love/ing	secure
enthusiastic	grateful	mellow	sensitive
exalted	gratification	merry	spellbound
excited	groovy	mirthful	splendid
exhilarated	happy	moved	stimulated
expansive	helpful	optimism	surprised
expectant	hopeful	overwhelmed	tender/ness
exuberant	inquisitive	overjoyed	thankful
fascinated	inspired	peaceful	thrilled
free	intense	pleasant/ure	touched
friendly	interested	proud	tranquil
fulfilled	intrigued	quiet	trust
gay	invigorated	radiant	warm
glad	involved	rapturous	wide-awake
gleeful	joy/ful/ous	refreshed	wonderful
glorious	jubilant	relief/ved	zest/ful
glowing	keyed-up	satisfied/faction	

Feelings likely to be present when wants aren't being satisfied

afraid	cross	exhausted	insensitive
aggravated	credulous	fatigued	intense
agitation	dejected	fear/ful	irate
alarm	depressed	fidgety	irked
aloof	despair	forlorn	irritated
angry	despondent	frightened	jealous
anguish	detached	frustrated	jittery
animosity	disappointed	furious	keyed-up
annoyance	discouraged	gloomy	lassitude
anxious	disgruntled	grief	lazy
apathetic	disgusted	guilty	let-down
apprehensive	disheartened	hate	lethargy
aroused	disinterested	heavy	listless
aversion	dislike	helpless	lonely
bad	dismayed	hesitant	mad
beat	displease	horrified	mean
bitter	disquieted	horrible	melancholy
blah	distressed	hostile	miserable
blue	disturbed	hot	mopy
bored	downcast	humdrum	nervous
breathless	downhearted	hurt	nettled
brokenhearted	dread	impatient	overwhelmed
chagrined	dull	indifferent	passive
cold	edgy	inert	perplexed
concerned	embarrassed	infuriated	pessimism/tic
confused	embittered	inquisitive	provoked
cool	exasperated	insecure	puzzled

12

rancorous	skeptical	terrified	unsteady
reluctant/ance	sleepy	thwarted	upset
repelled	sorrowful	tired	uptight
resentful	sorry	troubled	vexed/ation
restless	sour	uncomfortable	weary
sad	spiritless	unconcerned	withdrawn
scared	startled	uneasy	woeful
sensitive	surprised	unglued	worried
shaky	suspicion	unhappy	wretched
shocked	tepid	unnerved	

I periodically remind myself of the limitation of using words to describe feelings. A description of an experience, no matter how vivid, clear or artistic it is, is never the experience itself.

I'm learning that I'm alienated from my feelings when I
(1) use the word "feel" but follow it with my thoughts rather than my feelings (for example, "I feel that I am right.")
(2) use words that tell more what I think I am than how I feel (for example, "I feel inadequate.").
(3) use words that tell more what I think others are doing to me than that reveal how I'm feeling (for example, "I feel misunderstood.").

13

I am providing the following exercise for you to use to determine whether we are communicating about language that I believe heightens awareness of what we are feeling. I would like you to circle the number of the statements in which the speaker is *verbally* expressing feelings.

1. I feel I am being cheated.

2. I'm feeling tense right now and I don't know why.

3. I feel that you are misinterpreting me.

4. I'm thinking of going to the dentist this afternoon and feeling scared about it.

5. I would appreciate it if you would take out the garbage.

6. That was nice of you to do that.

7. I feel I am an impatient person.

8. I feel pushed around.

9. I feel good.

10. I'm not angry at you for what you did.

11. Your remark is confusing.

12. I'm irritated with myself for what I just did.

13. I feel dominated by you.

14. I am terrified whenever I'm around snakes.

15. I feel uncared for.

16. He annoys me when he is around.

17. I don't know how I feel.

18. I feel like shouting.

19. It's interesting that you said that.

20. I feel bad.

Following are my responses with which to compare yours.

1. *I do not hear a present feeling being verbally expressed. To do so the speaker might have said, "I'm angry because I believe you're cheating me."*

2. *I do hear a present feeling expressed.*

3. *I do not hear a present feeling being verbally expressed. To do so the speaker might have said, "I'm frustrated because I want you to interpret me differently."*

4. *I do hear a present feeling being expressed.*

5. *I do not hear a present feeling being verbally expressed. To do so the speaker might have said, "I'm feeling tense because of all the things I want to do today. I would appreciate it if you would take out the garbage."*

6. *I do not hear a present feeling being verbally expressed. To do so the speaker might have said, "I'm pleased that you did that."*

7. *I do not hear a present feeling being verbally expressed. To do so the speaker might have said, "I'm disgusted with myself because I'm saying I shouldn't be so impatient."*

8. *I do not hear a present feeling being verbally expressed. To do so the speaker ight have said, "I feel irritated because I'm interpreting you as pushing me around."*

9. *I would call this a "general" feeling. Note that it could mean that the speaker was happy, excited, warm, etc.*

10. *I do not hear a present feeling being expressed; rather I hear the person saying how s/he doesn't feel. To express feelings the speaker might have said, "I'm not angry at you for what you did; I'm disappointed because I didn't get what I wanted."*

11. *I do not hear a present feeling being verbally expressed. To do so the speaker might have said, "I'm confused because I don't understand your remark."*

12. *I do hear a present feeling being expressed.*

13. *I do not hear a present feeling being verbally expressed. To do so the speaker might have said, "I feel angry because I'm telling myself you have no right to dominate me."*

14. *I do not hear a present feeling being verbally expressed. I would describe it as a a generalization about how the person feels when around snakes, but not necessarily how the person was feeling at the moment the statement was made.*

15

15. *I do not hear a present feeling being verbally expressed.* To do so the speaker might have said, *"When you don't call for a week, I feel hurt because I interpret you as not caring for me."*

16. *I do not hear a present feeling being verbally expressed.* To do so the speaker might have said, *"I feel annoyed when he is around because I don't get the chance to talk that I would like to have."*

17. *I do not hear a present feeling being verbally expressed.* To do so the speaker might have said, *"I'm frustrated because I would like to be in touch with my feelings and I'm not."*

18. *I do not hear a present feeling being verbally expressed.* To express feelings the speaker might have said, *"I'm so happy I feel like shouting."*

19. *I do not hear a present feeling being verbally expressed.* To do so the speaker might have said, *"I'm excited that you said that because I had hoped for your agreement."*

20. *I would call this a "general" feeling. Note that the speaker could be feeling unahppy, guilty, angry, etc.*

16

Chapter Four

What we are valuing

I'd like to dig my soul
   out of the mess I see
     cluttering my mind.
Too much of life,
   too much of me,
     is getting left behind.

Programs in my head
   make me feel so dead
     and never bring a smile.
I'd like to tune in
   to a different channel
     but never seem to find the dial.

My head was filled
   with a million or more
     have to's, should's, and oughts.
So I spend my time
   and my energy
     unraveling my knots.

I've often been told
   that when things go bad
     "Find somebody to blame."
Philosophies like that
   can easily give
     living a bad name.

The third piece of information in empowering evaluations describes what we are valuing that contributes to our feeling as we do.

Our feelings result not from what we observe alone but also from how we react to what we observe. I first remember being aware of this when I was about 5 or 6 years-old. A friend of mine taught me, "Sticks and stones can break my bones, but names can never hurt me." How valuable I found that! It helped me realize that my feelings were not created by what others did but how I took what they did!

We take things as we do because of the values we bring to any situation. Sometimes our values are imbedded in what we imagine could happen. For example, I might feel afraid if I fail to observe my children brushing their teeth because I might imagine them getting cavities. Sometimes our values are imbedded in interpretations we make. For example, I might feel angry because I interpret someone as being thoughtless and inconsiderate.

Failing to be aware of the values contributing to our feeling as we do blinds us to the cultural programming we bring to situations.

A good deal of the cultural indoctrination we bring to conflicts does not support nonviolent ways of influencing people. In fact, much of it justifies explosive, competitive and violent actions. Joseph Parenti describes such internalized values:

There were other values we learned as supplements to our lessons in jingoism and authoritarianism. We learned that it was better to have a lot of money than very little – not that anyone ever quite put it that way, but we knew it was considered better to work in a big office than as a laborer, better to live in the starched antiseptic world of Dick and Jane than in fecund East Harlem. We were urged to 'study hard,' 'get ahead,' and 'better yourself,' and this betterment was almost always defined in terms of material advancement, winning out against others, gaining a more prestigious occupation and larger income, and rarely as dedication to the less fortunate, to social causes, social justice, and mutual betterment through cooperative

18

efforts. And never was it suggested that 'bettering yourself' might entail some essential changes in the systems of authority, property, and power that shaped our lives in ways we never appreciated.

(1973)

I find that when I'm conscious that such internalized learning is occurring I can prevent it from interferring with my ability to exchange resources and resolve differences nonviolently. Toward this end I find it helpful to explain my feelings with reference to a "because I" statement in which I acknowledge what I'm doing that is contributing to my feelings, e.g. "When you didn't ask me to go along with you, I felt hurt because I took it as a rejection." Not only do such statements alert me to the cultural programming operating within me, but they also reduce the possibility that others will hear my feelings as blame or "guilt tripping."

19

I am offering an exercise for you to use in determining whether we are communicating about how "because I" clauses can aid us in detecting what we are doing that contributes to our feeling as we do. I would like you to circle the number of the statement in which the speaker acknowledges the inner associations contributing to his/her feelings.

1. You make me angry when you spill milk on the table.

2. You scare me when you look like that.

3. I'm excited with the news you just told me because I want Jim to visit.

4. I'm hurt because you don't want to be with me tonight.

5. I'm pleased that you got an "A" in Science.

6. I'm feeling irritated because I just saw Mr. Jones spank a child.

7. I'm depressed with what I have accomplished this year because I interpret myself as inadequate for not having accomplished more.

8. When you hug me I feel tense.

9. I'm confused by your story.

10. I'm angry with you because I waited all day for you to call.

Hear are my responses to compare with yours:

1. I do not hear the speaker explaining the inner associations contributing to his/ her feelings. Contrast the statement as it was written with, "I feel angry when you spill milk on the table because I interpret you as careless and sloppy."

2. I do not hear the speaker explaining the inner associations contributing to his/ her feelings. Contrast the statement as it was written with, "I feel scared when you look at me like that because I think you might hurt me."

3. I do hear the speaker explaining the inner associations contributing to his/her feelings.

4. I do not hear the speaker explaining the inner associations contributing ot his/ her feelings. Contrast the statement as it was written with, "I'm hurt because I'm taking your not wanting to be with me tonight as a personal rejection."

5. *I do not hear the speaker explaining the inner associations contributing to his/her feelings. Contrast the statement as it was written with, "I'm pleased that you got an "A" in Science because I wanted you to get a sense of achievement."*

6. *I do not hear the speaker explaining the inner associations contributing to his/her feelings. Contrast the statement as it was written with, "I'm feeling irritated because I just saw Mr. Jones spank a child and I don't believe that people have a right to spank children."*

7. *I do hear the speaker explaining the inner associations contributing to his/her feelings.*

8. *I do not hear the speaker explaining the inner associations contributing to his/her feelings. Contrast the statement as it was written with, "When you hug me I feel tense because I often interpret you as wanting something from me."*

9. *I do not hear the speaker explaining the inner associations contributing to his/her feelings. Contrast the statement as it was written with, "I'm confused because I wanted to get the point of your story and I didn't."*

10. *I do not hear the speaker explaining the inner associations contributing to his/her feelings. Contrast the statement as it was written with, "I'm angry with you for not calling all day because I interpreted you as thoughtless for keeping me waiting."*

Chapter Five

What we are requesting

*Who do I want to do what right now
 to get us where I'd like us to be?
That's the awesome challenge
 ever confronting me.*

*A loving man I respect once said
 it would benefit you and me
if each of us were willing
 to sin courageously.*

*Choosing what I want to happen
 aware of my fallibility
is a risky path to follow
 but one I choose joyfully.*

*I'm able to choose my own destiny
 and march to the beat of my soul
when instead of being perfect
 being myself is my goal.*

The fourth piece of information in empowering evaluations expresses what we are requesting in positive action language. Using positive action language in making requests increases the likelihood that our requests will be honored. Positive action language refers to specific actions I'd like taken, e.g. "I'd like you to take your books back to the library this afternoon" or "I'd like you to agree to meet with me at least one hour a week for the next month." Most of us are familiar with the adage, "In unity there is strength." I would add to this, "In clarity there is strength." When I clarify exactly who I'd like to take what specific actions I'm more likely to get what I want than I am when my requests are enmeshed in a sea of rhetoric. Elinor Langer, a social activist in the 60's, describes what can happen when we get lost in rhetoric:

> If I regret anything it is that I was not clearheaded enough most of the time in the movement to have helped make it stronger or to prolong or reinforce its impact . . . It was as if the only way our vague political feelings about revolution and the system could express themselves was in general rhetorical language, and it was very important to say the right combination of words, have the right view . . .
> But in fact our words armored us against the very people we needed to have fighting on our side.

(1973)

Language of rhetoric buries the specific actions we'd like taken in vaguely defined abstractions, e.g. "I want you to accept me as I am," "I want you to respect my rights," "I want you to love me as much as I love you," "I want you to consider my opinion," "I want some understanding." Notice that use of the verb "to be" can easily obscure what we want to happen; for example, "I want you to be more cooperative" (or respectful, loving, etc.)

When I'm using positive action language I avoid telling people how I'd like them to feel or think unless I also recommend actions they might take in order to feel as I would like them to be able to. For example, if I say or think to myself, "I want to feel more comfortable in group situations than I do," I am not

23

likely to reach this objective unless I can also imagine some action likely to bring this about. Thus, I might add to the statement, "I want to feel more comfortable in group situations than I do" the statement, "so I am going to ask John what he does to bolster his confidence in group situations." Likewise, if I am talking to others, I want to avoid expressing wants containing reference only to how I want them to feel. Instead of saying only, "I want you to feel free to express yourself around me," I want to add, "I'd like you to tell me what I might do to make it easier for you to do so."

When I'm using positive action language I state what I do want, not simply what I don't want. It is the difference between creation and negation and between assertiveness and disobedience. If I say only what I don't want without also clarifying what I do want, my growth is limited. I recall a time when I was debating an issue on a television program in St. Louis with a gentleman whose political views are contrary to my own. The program was taped in the afternoon and shown in the evening. This provided me with an opportunity to watch myself on television. What a painful experience! There I was acting in ways that I deplore. I then expressed some "don't wants" to myself, saying, "if I'm ever debating issues in public again I don't want to do what I saw myself doing." I had three specific actions clearly in mind that I wanted to avoid. Two weeks later I was invited to continue my debate with the same gentleman. All the way to the studio I kept repeating to myself the three actions I didn't want to take. The program began and for ten seconds I didn't take the three actions. I didn't take any actions. I just sat there. I was clear about what I didn't want to do but I didn't know what I did want to do. I imagine you can guess what happened after the ten seconds. Yes, that's right. Not only did I begin to act in the ways I had vowed to stop but I seemed to make up for the lost ten seconds. This story reminds me of how important it is to think in terms of new alternatives whether it is my behavior or that of others I want changed.

24

When I am speaking with another person I like to remain aware of the difference in clarity between "I would like you to _____" statements and "I would like to _____" statements. For example, if I say to you, "I would like to get to know you better," you would know what my intentions were but you wouldn't know what I wanted you to do about this. Notice how much clearer I become if I add to such statements an "I'd like you to" statement that clarifies what I'm wanting from the person at that moment. Example: I'd like to get to know you better. I'd like you to tell me whether you'd be willing to go out to dinner with me Saturday."

What others believe our intentions (visions) are will also affect whether or not they will cooperate with our requests. Our intentions refer to what we would like to happen. Our requests are the "work" we would like to have done so that what we would like to have happen does happen. Nonviolent exchanges of resources and resolutions of differences are made possible when others believe our intentions are to nurture, educate, and protect and not to blame, punish, or dominate.

I offer the following exercise for you to see if we are communicating about expressing requests using positive action language. I would like you to circle the number of the statement in which requests are expressed using positive action language.

1. (Speaking with another person, hereafter abbreviated to swap) I want you to love me.

2. (swap) I don't want you calling me every day.

3. (thinking to oneself, hereafter abbreviated to tto) I want to feel affectionate toward you.

4. (swap) I want you to listen to me.

5. (swap) I want to tell you what happened to me today.

6. (tto) I want to call Janet now.

7. (tto) I don't want to complain as much as I have been.

8. (swap) I want to spend more time with you.

9. (swap) I would like you to be honest with me.

10. (swap) Do I talk too much?

11. (tto) I want to be a success.

12. (swap) I wish you would respect my authority on this matter.

13. (swap) Before you leave for school I want you to say to yourself, "I'm not going to forget to take out the garbage when I come home."

14. (swap) I would like you to bring your bicycle in out of the rain.

15. (swap) I would like for you to tell me whether you have seen the movie, "Lenny."

16. (swap) I want you to understand me.

17. (swap) Why did you hit him?

18. (swap) I would like you to tell me if I'm too fat.

19. (swap) I want to hear more from you at meetings.

20. (swap) I don't want you telling me what to do.

21. (swap) I would like you to call me at least once a month.

22. (swap) I don't want you to call him names.

23. (swap) I want you to tell me you love me.

24. (swap) I would like you to think before you act.

Hear are my responses with which to compare yours:

1. *I would not say this want is expressed in positive action language because of the word "love." Contrast with, "I want you to tell me you love me," or "I want you to agree to spend at least some time alone with me each week."*

2. *I would not say this want is expressed in positive action language because it states what the speaker does not want but does not add what s/he does want. Contrast with, "I'd like you to call me no more than once each day."*

3. *I would not say this want is expressed in positive action language because it expresses a feeling but not an action. Contrast with, "I want to list three things I tell myself about Janet that prevent me from liking her."*

4. *I would not say this want is expressed in positive action language because of the word "listen." Contrast with, "I'd like you to paraphrase what you hear me saying before reacting."*

5. *I see this want expressed in positive action language.*

6. *I see this want expressed in positive action language.*

7. *I would not say this want is expressed in positive action language because it states what the speaker does not want but does not add what s/he does want. Also, I would not call the word "complain" an observable word. Contrast with, "I want to list at least one thing I like about what Jack has been doing."*

8. *I would not say this is expressed in positive action language because it is addressed to another person and uses an "I want to" structure without following with an "I want you to.. component. Contrast with, "I'd like to spend more time with you. I'd like you to tell me how you feel about this."*

9. *I would not say this want is expressed in positive action language because of the words "be honest." Contrast with, "I'd like you to tell me what I've been doing that you don't like."*

10. *I would not say this question is expressed in positive action language because*

27

of the words "too much." Contrast with, "I'd like you to tell me if I'm talking more than you would like."

11. I would not say this want is expressed in positive action language because of the words "to be a success." Contrast with, "I want to sell 10,000 copies of this book."

12. I would not say this want is expressed in positive action language because of the words "respect my authority." Contrast with, "I'd like you to paraphrase what you heard my reasons being for not wanting you to. Then I'd like you to tell me your feelings about what I said."

13. I see this want expressed in positive action language.

14. I see this want expressed in positive action language.

15. I see this want expressed in positive action language.

16. I would not say this want is expressed in positive action language because of the word "understand." Contrast with, "I'd like you to demonstrate your understanding by writing a sentence where the subject and predicate agree."

17. I would not say this want is expressed in positive action language because of the word "why." Contrast with, "I'd like you to tell me what you were feeling when you hit him and what you told yourself that made you angry."

18. I would not say this want is expressed in positive action language because of the words, "too fat." Contrast with, "I'd like you to tell me if you would interpret me as too fat."

19. I would not say this want is expressed in positive action language because it is addressed to another person and uses an "I want to" structure without following with an "I want you to" component. Contrast with, "I'd like to hear more from you in meetings. I'd like you to tell me what I might do to make it easier for you to participate."

20. I would not say this want is expressed in positive action language because it states what the speaker does not want but does not add what s/he does want. Contrast with, "I'd like you to tell me what you want, not what you think I should do."

21. I see this want expressed in positive action language.

22. I would not say this want is expressed in positive action language because it states what the speaker does not want but does not add what s/he does want. Contrast with, "I'd like you to tell him how you feel and what you want without calling him names."

23. I see this want expressed in positive action language.

23. *I see this want expressed in positive action language.*

24. *I would not say this want is expressed in positive action language because of the word, "think." Contrast with, "I want you to paraphrase back the possible disadvantages I see to what you are proposing."*

Chapter Six

Receiving Empowering Evaluations

I want to give you
the gift of empathy
and rid myself of stereotypes
limiting what I see.

It's taken me a while
but I realize at last
how much I miss the present
with eyes fogged with the past.

So if I take some time
before I answer you
I'm clearing away the projections
that dehumanize my view.

Exchanging resources and resolving differences nonviolently requires that we be equally adept at receiving empowering evaluations as we are offering them.

Receiving empowering evaluations involves accurately receiving:

what others are observing

what others are feeling about what they are observing

what others are valuing that contributes to their feeling as they do

what others are requesting

I enjoy communicating with people who have the literacy and trust necessary to clearly communicate these four pieces of information. Frequently, however, I find myself communicating with people who lack such literacy and/or trust. When this is the case I have found two things I can do to elicit the four pieces of information. First, I can request the information preceding the request with what is going on within me that leads me to make the request. For example, if someone says to me, "You are too cold and aloof." I might say, "I'm confused about what I'm doing that is coming across that way. I'd appreciate your telling me what I'm doing or not doing that is coming across to you as cold and aloof." Unless we have a pretty sound relationship I've found that if I ask questions like, "What are you talking about?" or "What have or haven't I done?", the person I'm asking such questions to is likely to misinterpret my reasons for asking the question and see me as being defensive or cross-examining them.

Another way of receiving the four pieces of information would be to paraphrase and check the accuracy of my paraphrase with the speaker. By paraphrasing I let the person know how I've interpreted the messages communicated to me and provide an opportunity for the person to correct me if I have misinterpreted them.

The kind of paraphrasing I do often takes forms such as "Are you reacting to _____?" or "Are you feeling_____because

31

you _____ ?" or "Would you like me to _____?"

Some rules of thumb that I follow in choosing when to paraphrase verbally are:

(a) Speakers give me some indication that they want reassurance that their message has been received accurately. This indication often takes the form of the speaker asking, "Is that clear?" or "Do you know what I mean?"

(b) I am not certain that I have accurately guessed what observations, feelings or wants the other person is expressing and I want verification before reacting.

(c) I would want someone to paraphrase if I had expressed the message. I know how vulnerable I feel when I openly reveal myself and how good it feels when others paraphrase. Therefore, if others express a deeply personal message to me, I might paraphrase even if they do not give specific indication that they want me to and I'm fairly confident I've understood.

Here is an exercise to aid you in determining whether we are communicating about the type of paraphrasing that I believe facilitates receiving the four pieces of information. I would like you to circle the numbers of the following situations where Person B is responding in a way that is consistent with that which I have been describing.

1. A: In my opinion , the best store to shop at in town is National.
   B: That's ridiculous. Kroger's prices are lower.

2. A: I think you made a mistake selling your car.
   B: (Feeling confident that she heard what A has just said and that A is satisfied with her understanding) I don't agree.

3. A: For me the movies on television are disturbed by the commercial interruptions.
   B: Are you saying you think the movies lose the impact the writers and directors intended when commercials interrupt the sequence?

4. A: It seems to me that you spend an inordinate amount of time studying.
   B: Are you thinking that I should spend more time studying?

5. A; I think Sir Laurence Olivier did his best performance when acting Hamlet.
   B: Are you saying you are capable of making this judgment?

6. A: You're the most selfish person I've ever met!
   B: Why do you say that?

7. A: You're overgenerous.
   B: Are you speaking of the size of my gift to Dorothy?

8. A: That was stupid of you.
   B: Are you annoyed because you think I should know better than to have misspelled that word?

9. A: I'm disgusted with you for not coming home for the holidays.
   B: Are you saying you're disgusted because I told you I was not coming home for the holidays?

10. A: I get bored when you tell such long stories.
    B: Are you saying my talking too much bores you?

11. A: You're so unaffectionate.
    B: Are you saying you would like me to be more affectionate?

12. A: You're too fat.
    B: Are you saying I should lose weight?

13. A: I wish you would be more conscientious about getting to work on time.
    B: Are you saying you would like me to agree to get to work on time from now on?

14. A: I'm excited with the possibility of your helping us in the election.
    B: Sounds like you're excited about the possibility of my helping you in this election but this won't be possible.

Here are my responses with which to compare yours:

1. *I do not see this as consistent. Contrast with, "Are you saying you enjoy shopping at National more than at any other store?"*

2. *I do see this as consistent.*

3. *I do see this as consistent.*

4. *I see this as consistent even through Person B has misinterpreted A. The purpose of the paraphrase is to give Person A a chance to correct possible misinterpretation and this paraphrase would provide that opportunity.*

5. *I do not see this as consistent because Person B is not guessing at what Person A is observing, feeling, thinking or wanting. Contrast with, "So in your estimation Laurence Olivier's greatest performance was Hamlet?"*

6. *I do not see this form of question as consistent; note that it neither guesses at what A might be observing, feeling, thinking or wanting nor is it an expression of Person B's wants expressed in positive action language. Contrast with, "Are you reacting to my not wanting to loan you my car?" or, "I'm confused; I'd like you to tell me what I did that you are reacting to."*

7. *I do see this as consistent.*

8. *I do see this as consistent.*

9. *I do not see this as consistent because the "because clause" does not clarify what A's inner associations are that are contributing to Person A's feeling and implies that Person B's behavior made Person A feel as he does. I believe this differentiation can be very helpful in preventing oneself from falling into the trap of thinking one can cause other peoples' feelings. Contrast this paraphrase with the one in Number 8 and also contrast with, "Are you saying you're disgusted because you think family members should be together for holidays?"*

10. *I do not see this as consistent because Person B paraphrased a confusion of ob-*

servation and evaluation and used the passive voice in referring to Person A's feelings. Contrast with, "When I tell such a long story, do you feel impatient because you want to insure that we have time to finish our business?"

11. I do not see this as consistent because Person B did not paraphrase Person A's wants using positive action language. Contrast with, "Are you saying you'd like me to kiss you when I come home?"

12. I do not see this as consistent. Contrast with, "Are you feeling worried because you think my weight jeopardizes my health and would you like me to find a diet I'm willing to stick with?"

13. I do see this as consistent.

14. I do not see this as consistent because Person B starts off by paraphrasing but shifts to his reaction without giving Person A a chance to correct his paraphrase. Contrast with, "Sounds like you're excited about the possibility of my helping you in this election. Is that right?"

Bibliography

Johnson, Wendell. *Living With Change.* New York: Harper & Row, 1972.

Langer, Elinor. "Notes for Next Time -- a Memoir of the 1960's," Working Papers, Vol. No. 3, Fall, 1973.

Parenti, Michael. "Politics of the Classroom," in Social Policy, Vol. 7, No. 1, July/August, 1973.

Additional Resources

Craig, James and Marguerite. *Synergic Power.* Berkeley, Ca: Proactive Press, 1974.

Lyons, Gracie. *Constructive Criticism.* Oakland, CA: IRT Press, 1977.

Marshall B. Rosenberg coordinates the Center for Nonviolent Communication, a network providing opportunities for people to develop and strengthen the communication skills described in this manual.

Marshall received a Ph.D. in clinical psychology from the University of Wisconsin in 1961 and was accorded diplomate status from the American Board of Examiners in Professional Psychology in 1966.

FROM
NEW SOCIETY
PUBLISHERS